FROM *Chaos* TO CALM

A GUIDE TO MANAGING DISCIPLINE AND FOSTERING A POSITIVE SCHOOL ENVIRONMENT

DR. GREGORY NUNLEY JR.

DORRANCE PUBLISHING CO
EST. 1920
PITTSBURGH, PENNSYLVANIA 15238

Dorrance Publishing Co
585 Alpha Drive
Suite 103
Pittsburgh, PA 15238
Visit our website at *www.dorrancebookstore.com*

ISBN: 979-8-89127-565-2
eISBN: 979-8-89127-063-3

To my cherished wife, Camishe, and our beloved children, Gregory III, Aniya, and Jasmine: This book stands as a testament to your unwavering love and support during my two-decade-long journey in education. As my foundation, you have filled my life with strength and encouragement. With immense gratitude, I dedicate this work to you and celebrate this milestone together.

For Information:

GNJ Impact & Innovation LLC
Fishers, Indiana 46038

gregorynunleyjr.net

CONTENTS

Introduction

Creating a positive school environment is more critical than ever in today's dynamic educational landscape. When students feel safe, supported, and respected, they are more likely to engage in learning, develop strong relationships, and achieve their full potential. As an experienced educator with a leadership, advising, and engagement background, I have spent my career working in high-poverty and over-populated schools. Despite these challenges, I have witnessed the incredible potential for growth and improvement that can be unlocked when schools effectively manage discipline concerns and foster a supportive atmosphere.

Throughout my journey as an assistant principal, principal, and now director of secondary education, I have been devoted to enhancing the learning environment for students by addressing disciplinary issues, supporting teachers, and expanding the services offered by our guidance department. I am particularly proud of my accomplishments in reducing discipline referrals, partnering with teachers to provide additional instructional support, restructuring the RTI process, and implementing innovative strategies to improve student outcomes.

This book synthesizes my experiences and expertise, providing a comprehensive guide to creating a positive school environment by effectively managing discipline concerns. In it, I outline ten essential components crucial for meeting our educational goals, despite the challenges posed by high-poverty and overpopulated schools. These components range from fostering a positive school culture to understanding schedules and building structures, maximizing resources, and nurturing strong relationships

with students and parents. This book is the culmination of my years of experience and presents a comprehensive framework for effectively managing school discipline concerns. Drawing on my successes and challenges, as well as the expertise of fellow educators, these ten identified components can help schools create a positive environment conducive to learning and growth.

In the following chapters, we will delve into each of these components, examining their importance and providing practical strategies for implementation. By consistently implementing these ten components, my team and I have reduced suspensions, expulsions, and teacher referrals, ultimately creating a more positive and effective learning environment for all students. I invite you to explore these strategies with me. Together, we can transform your school into a nurturing, supportive, and successful educational community that empowers students to thrive, regardless of their circumstances.

CHAPTER ONE

DEVELOPING A POSITIVE SCHOOL CULTURE

A positive school culture is the foundation of a thriving educational community. The invisible yet powerful force shapes how students, staff, and parents perceive, experience, and engage with the learning environment. A positive school culture promotes inclusivity, respect, and a sense of belonging for all community members. This chapter will delve into the essential components of a positive school culture, explaining the importance of each element and how they collectively contribute to creating an empowering and supportive atmosphere.

1. *Developing and Communicating the School's Vision and Mission*

The school's vision and mission are the guiding principles that articulate the educational community's core values, goals, and aspirations. Schools establish a shared sense of purpose and direction by clearly defining and communicating the vision and mission. This unified understanding fosters a sense of belonging and inclusivity, as all community members can identify with and contribute to realizing these common goals. Regularly revisiting and reiterating the vision and mission keeps the community aligned and motivated, ensuring that every decision and action is rooted in these guiding principles.

A vision statement is a concise, inspiring declaration of an organization's long-term goals and aspirations. It is a guiding principle for the organization's strategic planning, decision-making, and overall direction. A well-crafted vision statement provides a clear picture of what the organization aims to achieve and helps motivate and unite

employees, stakeholders, and the community around a shared purpose. A vision statement should be aspirational, reflecting the organization's core values and beliefs and articulating a desirable future state that the organization is working towards. It is important to note that a vision statement differs from a mission statement. While a mission statement focuses on the organization's purpose and activities, a vision statement looks forward to the desired future.

Here is an example of a vision statement built around building a positive school environment.

School Vision Statement:
Our vision is to create a nurturing, inclusive, and dynamic learning environment that fosters a sense of belonging, collaboration, and respect among all stakeholders. We strive to empower students to reach their full potential by providing the necessary tools, resources, and support. We are committed to fostering positive relationships, promoting academic success, and cultivating responsible, empathetic, well-rounded citizens.

A mission statement is a brief, clear, and concise declaration of an organization's core purpose, values, and objectives. It guides the organization's actions and decision-making processes by providing a framework for its goals, strategies, and priorities. The mission statement outlines what the organization does, whom it serves, and how it achieves its purpose.

A well-crafted mission statement helps to communicate the organization's identity, values, and priorities to employees, stakeholders, and the public. It creates a shared understanding of the organization's purpose and instills a

sense of direction and focus. Unlike a vision statement, which outlines the organization's aspirational long-term goals, a mission statement focuses more on the present, describing the organization's fundamental purpose and primary activities.

Here is an example of a mission statement built around building a positive school environment.

School Mission Statement:

Our mission is to provide a comprehensive education centered around our ten core areas to ensure every student's positive and enriching school experience. We are committed to promoting a culture of inclusivity, respect, and collaboration by fostering open communication and teamwork among students, staff, and parents. We are dedicated to maximizing our resources, implementing adequate supervision and classroom expectations, and creating a safe and engaging environment that supports student growth and development. By cultivating strong relationships with students and parents, we strive to create a supportive and connected community that empowers everyone to thrive academically, socially, and emotionally.

2. *Encouraging Collaboration and Teamwork*

A positive school culture thrives on collaboration and teamwork. When staff, students, and parents work together in the spirit of cooperation, they create an environment where collective intelligence and shared responsibility become the norm. This collaborative approach fosters a sense of mutual support, trust, and accountability, allowing all community members to feel valued and empowered. By facilitating opportunities for collaboration, schools can harness their members' diverse talents, perspectives, and experiences, leading to more innovative solutions and tremendous overall success.

Creating a team that works together successfully does not simply happen because you put a group of educated individuals together. This occurs a lot in schools. An example is putting all the math teachers together to develop common assessments without establishing the norms for the group and identifying their roles. This typically leads to a long, drawn-out process where the frustration impacts the team's ability to function. Ultimately the buy-in for utilizing the common assessment is lost. I have witnessed grade-level teams planning the student incentive trips for the year, yet they need help to complete those tasks because the group cannot agree on the parameters for students to participate. Creating a successful team requires understanding each member's roles and responsibilities, fostering open communication, promoting compromise, navigating disagreements, and providing feed-back with grace and understanding. Since basketball is my favorite sport, I will use a basketball team analogy as a reference point; we will explore how these elements can be applied within a school community to encourage collaboration and teamwork.

a. Define team members' roles and responsibilities.

On a basketball team, each player has a specific position and responsibility. For instance, point guards are responsible for directing the team's offense, while centers focus on rebounding and defending the rim. Similarly, each member has a unique role and responsibility in a school community. Teachers are responsible for providing instruction, administrators ensure the smooth functioning of the school, and parents support their children's learning at home. When everyone understands their roles and works together, the school community functions effectively and efficiently. When forming a team, clarify what role each team member will play. Everyone should have a clear understanding of what is and what is not expected of them.

b. Foster open communication.

Effective communication is crucial for successful teamwork. On a basketball team, players must constantly communicate with one another to execute plays and coordinate their defense. Likewise, open communication is essential in a school community. Staff, students, and parents should be encouraged to share their thoughts, concerns, and ideas openly and honestly. This open dialogue helps build trust and fosters a sense of shared ownership in the school's success. When forming a team, model what open communication looks like for everyone. Discuss the different mediums in which communication will occur. Discuss things like email communication, text communication, and group communication. It is essential to talk about tone and body language and how it is easy to misperceive things that are said simply by the way it is stated.

c. Promote compromise.

In any collaborative environment, compromise is often necessary. As basketball players must pass the ball to a teammate with a better scoring opportunity, school community members must also be willing to compromise to reach shared goals. By promoting a culture of compromise, schools can encourage all members to work together effectively and demonstrate flexibility in pursuing the greater good. When creating a team, discuss that you will probably only get some of what you want. Figure out what the process for deciding is. Will you vote, or is there some other method of determining?

d. Navigate disagreements.

Disagreements are inevitable in any team setting. In basketball, players might argue over a missed shot or defensive assignment. In a school community, disputes can arise over various issues, such as curriculum decisions or resource allocation. The key to navigating disagreements is to address them constructively, focusing on the problem rather than personalizing conflicts. Schools can ensure that differences are resolved to promote growth and learning by fostering a culture of respect and understanding.

e. Provide feedback with grace and understanding.

Constructive feedback is essential for continuous improvement and growth. On a basketball team, coaches and teammates provide feedback to help players refine their skills and better contribute to the team's success. Similarly, in a school community, feedback should be provided with grace and understanding. This includes offering praise and encouragement for accomplishments and constructive criticism to help individuals learn and grow. By cultivating a culture of supportive feedback, schools can empower their members to take risks, learn from their mistakes, and achieve their full potential.

By incorporating these elements into the school community, schools can foster a culture of collaboration and teamwork that supports their collective success. When all school community members work together with a shared purpose and a commitment to cooperation, they can create an environment where everyone succeeds, and the school's goals are more readily achieved.

3. *Fostering Open Communication and Feedback*

Open communication and feedback are essential to the growth and development of a positive school culture. Schools can identify and address concerns, celebrate achievements, and continuously refine their practices by encouraging dialogue and transparency among students, teachers, and administrators. This open exchange of ideas and information also builds trust and respect, as all school community members feel heard and valued. By cultivating a culture of open communication, schools can foster a sense of ownership and shared responsibility for improving the learning environment.

There are times when schools ask for feedback but will disregard it because it does not fit the narrative they want it to. I recall that once in a meeting, we reviewed the input of some presentations presented to staff. Most of the feedback was positive, but a small percentage expressed concerns with the quality of the content within the presentations. In the meeting, the group began to pick apart the source of the feedback instead of considering their concerns. When the group in the meeting discounted that feedback, we lost an opportunity to gain experience and create better overall presentations for all staff. We may only sometimes like what we hear, but it is important to encourage open communication and reflect on all the information received.

4. *Creating an Environment of Respect, Kindness, and Empathy*

At the heart of a positive school culture is a commitment to treating every school community member with respect, kindness, and empathy.

By modeling these values and actively fostering an environment where they are practiced and celebrated, schools can create a safe and supportive atmosphere where all members can thrive. This nurturing environment encourages students to take risks, embrace challenges, and develop the resilience necessary for lifelong learning and personal growth. Here are several examples of what this looks like in a school community.

a. Anti-bullying programs: A school can implement anti-bullying programs and workshops to educate students, teachers, and staff about the harmful effects of bullying and how to promote a positive school culture. Without these programs, bullying can become a pervasive issue, leading to higher rates of depression, anxiety, and dropout among students. The Anti-Defamation League is an organization I have worked with that provides many free resources on bullying.

b. Conflict resolution training: Schools can train students, teachers, and staff on effective conflict resolution techniques and communication skills. This enables them to address disagreements and misunderstandings respectfully and empathetically. Without proper conflict resolution training, conflicts can escalate, causing emotional distress and harm to relationships within the school community.

c. Teacher-student mentoring programs: A school can establish mentorship programs where teachers and students are paired to build trust and develop a supportive relationship. These connections help students feel valued and understood. With such mentorship programs, students may feel connected to the school community, leading to higher engagement and academic achievement. Two of the best mentoring programs I have used are "Young Men of Purpose" and "Young Women of Purpose," authored by Roy K. Dobbs. The program's fully digital curriculums explains and guides facilitators through mentoring.

d. Inclusive curriculum: Implementing an inclusive curriculum that reflects and honors the diversity of the student body helps students feel respected and valued. Without an inclusive curriculum, students from diverse backgrounds may not feel supported, leading to disengagement and lower academic performance.

e. Encouraging acts of kindness: Schools can create initiatives that encourage and celebrate acts of kindness, such as a "Kindness Wall" where students and staff can post notes recognizing kind acts. These initiatives are necessary for acts of kindness to be noticed, and students may learn the importance of empathy and compassion. At one school I visited, they utilized several bulletin boards and had kindness trees where students could write acts of kindness from staff and students on a leaf that would be later placed on the kindness tree for everyone to see.

Schools risk fostering a hostile culture that can have severe consequences for students, teachers, and staff without creating an environment of respect, kindness, and empathy. These consequences can include:

i.   Increased bullying and harassment, leading to emotional distress and poor mental health among students.

ii. Poor academic performance and disengagement due to students feeling unsupported and disconnected from their school community.

iii. Increased conflicts and unresolved issues among students, teachers, and staff, causing a breakdown in relationships and trust.

iv. Decreased overall well-being and personal growth for students, as they may need to develop the necessary skills and resilience to navigate life's challenges.

v.   Lower teacher morale and higher staff turnover due to the school community's hostile atmosphere and lack of support.

5. *Offering Regular Professional Development Opportunities*

Investing in staff's professional growth and development is crucial to cultivating a positive school culture. By providing regular opportunities for professional development, schools demonstrate a commitment to continuous improvement and empower staff to refine their skills, expand their knowledge, and stay current with best practices. This commitment to professional growth elevates the quality of teaching and learning. It fosters a culture of collaboration and innovation, as the staff is inspired to share and apply their newfound insights.

6. *Developing and Enforcing Clear Values and Expectations*

Establishing and enforcing a clear set of values and expectations for all students and staff is essential to a positive school culture. These expectations are the foundation for behavior, work ethic, and interpersonal interactions, ensuring all school community members understand and adhere to the same exacting standards. Schools create a fair and equitable environment for all students and staff by consistently upholding these values and expectations.

If a school does not develop and enforce clear values and expectations, it can lead to a range of negative consequences that can adversely impact the school's culture. Some of these consequences include the following:

a. Inconsistency and confusion: Without clear values and expectations, students and staff may not be confident of their expectations. This can lead to inconsistent behavior, performance, and communication, creating confusion and frustration.

b. Lack of accountability: Holding individuals accountable for their actions or performance becomes difficult without clear expectations. This can lead to a lack of responsibility, diminished motivation, and a sense of complacency.

c. Increased behavioral issues: Students may be more likely to engage in disruptive or inappropriate actions without established expectations for behavior. This can result in a less conducive learning environment and increased disciplinary concerns.

d. Decreased sense of belonging and engagement: When values and expectations are unclear, students and staff may need help to connect with the school's culture and feel a sense of belonging. This can lead to disengagement, reduced participation in school activities, and a lower sense of school pride.

e. Unequal treatment: Without a consistent set of values and expectations, there is a risk of unfair or unequal treatment of students and staff. This can lead to resentment, discrimination, and an unhealthy school climate.

f. Lower academic achievement: A lack of clear expectations can hinder students' academic progress. Students may need help to understand what is required of them; if they do not, it will lead to lower levels of achievement and a decline in the overall quality of education.

To prevent these adverse outcomes, schools must develop and enforce clear values and expectations that guide the behavior and performance of all school community members. By doing so, they create a positive, inclusive, and high-performing school culture where everyone can succeed.

7. *Promote character education and social-emotional learning programs.*

Integrating character education and social-emotional learning programs into the curriculum is another critical strategy for developing a positive school culture. These programs help students develop essential life skills, such as empathy, resilience, and self-regulation, contributing to their overall well-being and success. By promoting the development of these skills, schools can foster a positive school culture that supports the holistic growth of students and prepares them for all challenges that may come their way.

In conclusion, developing a positive school culture is crucial for the success and well-being of all students, staff, and community members. This chapter has highlighted the key elements that contribute to a thriving educational community, including establishing and communicating the school's mission and vision; encouraging collaboration and teamwork; fostering open communication and feedback, creating an environment of respect, kindness, and empathy; offering regular professional development opportunities; developing and enforcing clear values and expectations; and promoting character education and social-emotional learning programs.

By prioritizing these essential components, schools can create an empowering and supportive atmosphere that cultivates a sense of belonging, inclusivity, and respect. A positive school culture is a foundation for a high-performing, engaged, and connected community where all members can succeed academically, socially, and emotionally. As schools evolve and adapt to the ever-changing education landscape, it is vital to consistently assess and refine the strategies used to build and maintain a positive school culture, ensuring all stakeholders' ongoing success and growth.

Items to Consider:

1. Creating and implementing a clear, concise, and inspiring vision statement that outlines the school's long-term goals and aspirations is essential.

2. The significance of crafting a mission statement that focuses on the school's core purpose, values, and objectives, helping to guide actions and decision-making processes.

3. The ongoing process of revisiting and reiterating the school's mission and vision, ensuring that the educational community remains aligned and motivated towards achieving common goals.

Reflection Questions:

1. How can we effectively communicate and reinforce our school's vision and mission to all educational community members, including students, staff, and local businesses?

2. How can we engage all stakeholders in developing and revising the school's vision and mission statements to ensure that they genuinely reflect the needs and aspirations of the community?

3. How can we regularly evaluate the effectiveness of our vision and mission statements in guiding the school's actions and decisions and maintaining a positive school culture?

CHAPTER TWO

UNDERSTAND YOUR MASTER SCHEDULE AND BELL SCHEDULE

Quality master and bell schedules significantly influence a positive and productive learning environment. An effective master schedule ensures that all students can access the courses, resources, and support needed to succeed. A well-structured bell schedule helps maintain order and minimize disruptions throughout the school day. In this chapter, we will explore the essential elements of both master and bell schedules and guide how to design and implement these schedules to optimize the overall educational experience for students and staff.

If school culture is the heartbeat of a school, then the master and bell schedule is the brain of the operation. Master schedules are complex systems that ensure the functionality of the school. When creating a master and bell schedule, several factors need to be considered. The first is what version of a master schedule your school has and what you are considering changing it to.

Block master schedules are a school scheduling system that organizes the school day into larger blocks, typically ranging from 60 to 120 minutes. This scheduling method allows for longer, uninterrupted class periods, enabling teachers and students to engage in more profound, focused learning experiences.

Block scheduling often involves rotating classes throughout the week, with students attending a subset of their courses daily. For example, a school might use an "A/B" block schedule, where students follow one set of classes on "A" days and a different group of classes on "B" days. This rotation allows for fewer class periods per day, reducing the number of transitions and disruptions.

Some benefits of block master scheduling include the following:

1. Increased instructional time: Longer class periods allow for more in-depth exploration of topics and enable teachers to employ various instructional strategies, such as project-based learning or group work.

2. Reduced transitions: With fewer classes per day, students experience fewer transitions between classes, leading to less time spent in hallways and more time for learning.

3. Greater flexibility: Block scheduling provides opportunities for interdisciplinary instruction, as teachers can collaborate and integrate lessons across subjects within the extended class periods.

4. Enhanced focus: Students and teachers can concentrate on fewer subjects daily, allowing for deeper engagement and understanding of the material.

5. Improved teacher-student relationships: The extended class time in block scheduling allows for more individualized attention and personalized learning experiences, fostering stronger connections between teachers and students.

However, block scheduling may also present challenges, such as difficulties in maintaining student engagement for extended periods or the need for teachers to adapt their lesson plans and instructional strategies to fit the extended class time. Overall, the effectiveness of block master scheduling depends on the school's ability to implement the system thoughtfully, considering the specific needs and goals of its students and staff.

Traditional master schedules are a school scheduling system that organizes the school day into shorter, fixed-length class periods, typically 40 to 60 minutes. This scheduling method divides the school day into a set number of periods, with students attending each of their courses every day.

Some key features of traditional master scheduling include:

1. Consistency: Students follow the same schedule daily, attending all their classes for shorter periods. This consistency allows for a predictable routine, benefiting students who flourish in the structure.

2. Regular exposure to subjects: Since students attend each class daily, they receive continuous reinforcement of concepts and skills across all subjects, which can help maintain momentum and aid retention.

3. More class periods per day: Traditional scheduling typically involves more class periods than block scheduling, which can be advantageous for covering a broader range of subjects or incorporating elective courses.

4. Easier scheduling: Traditional master schedules are generally simpler to create and manage, involving fewer variations and complexities than block scheduling.

However, traditional master scheduling also presents some challenges:

1. Limited instructional time: Shorter class periods can constrain teachers' ability to delve deeply into topics or employ various instructional strategies, such as project-based learning or extensive group work.

2. Increased transitions: With more daily classes, students experience more transitions between classes, contributing to lost instructional time and potential disruptions.

3. Less flexibility: Traditional scheduling may offer different opportunities for interdisciplinary instruction or collaborative planning than block scheduling.

Ultimately, the choice between traditional and block master scheduling depends on the school's specific goals, needs, and priorities. Both systems have advantages and disadvantages, and it's essential to consider the unique characteristics of the school community when making a scheduling decision.

1. *Ensure Smooth Transitions between Classes with Staggered Passing Times*

One essential element of a well-functioning bell schedule is to minimize crowding and misbehavior during class transitions. By staggering passing times, schools can reduce the number of students in hallways and shared areas at any given time, allowing for a more orderly and calmer environment. This strategy not only helps prevent potential incidents but also allows for smoother transitions, reducing stress and anxiety for students and staff. There is also the benefit of pooling your resources into one specific area, allowing for more supervision and coverage of the building. Unfortunately, all schools cannot have staggered passing periods, so utilizing things like teacher teaming where all students' classes are in the same hallway can limit traffic flow to other areas. Locker placement can be more specific to the hallway so that students do not need to leave their designated area.

2. *Schedule Brain Breaks or Recess Times*

Students need time throughout the day to release energy, socialize, and regroup. By incorporating brain breaks and recess times into the bell schedule, schools can ensure that students have opportunities to relax and recharge. This downtime is crucial for maintaining focus, reducing stress, and promoting overall well-being. Furthermore, these breaks can contribute to a more positive school culture by fostering healthy social interactions and providing opportunities for students to engage in physical activity.

3. *Allocate Advisory or Homeroom Periods or Enrichment Time*

Advisory, homeroom, or enrichment periods are essential to a comprehensive master schedule. These dedicated periods allow students to connect with a consistent adult mentor who can provide guidance, support, and encouragement. Advisory, homeroom, or enrichment periods also create opportunities for relationship-building and collaboration among students, contributing to a sense of belonging and community within the school. This also can be utilized as an opportunity to provide some tier-two interventions for students needing extra curriculum support.

During my final year as an assistant principal and continuing in my first year as principal, the teachers and I collaborated to create unique student activity offerings. During our 30-minute enrichment time, teachers created opportunities such as math games, money management, yoga training, crafting craze, 3D printing, athletic training, music and sounds, and others. Students had the opportunity

to make a selection for each academic quarter. I used my ECA accounts to pay for materials and received donations from several churches and local businesses. I formed an enrichment committee of teachers, counselors, and administrators. We also received feedback from our student council. Beginning in January and throughout the summer, we planned and collaborated with staff on course offerings and resources needed. I was able to get all the courses uploaded into our school management system. We sent home to the parents and students the course offerings for each quarter and allowed them to select their top two choices for each quarter. Initially, it was a lot of work and planning, but once we laid the foundation, it became a staple of the master schedule and something our students looked forward to every year.

4. *Ensure the Master Schedule Is Designed to Minimize Student Idle Time and Transitions*

To optimize learning and minimize disruptions, it is essential to design the master schedule to reduce idle time and unnecessary transitions for students. This includes group classes with similar subject areas or grade levels and organizing class periods to minimize students' time moving between various locations. By streamlining the master schedule, schools can create a more efficient and focused learning environment. Every year I made sure to walk the building and time myself as a reminder to determine how many minutes a student needed to get from one class to the next. It usually took about three minutes, even with a stop at the locker. Depending on the size of your school, this could be longer, but the critical point is that you need to test it out before the beginning of the school year. Print off several students' schedules and walk them during the summer and then again during the school year. This is an excellent way to assess your transition times. Too much time can lead to many problems, so getting this right is essential.

5. *Communicate the Bell Schedule to All Students and Staff*

Effective communication is critical to the successful implementation of any schedule. Ensure all students and staff know the bell schedule, including start and end times for each class period, passing times, breaks, and any unique events or assemblies. Providing this information in a clear and accessible format, such as on the school website or in a student handbook, is essential for maintaining consistency and order throughout the day.

6. *Use Visual and Auditory Cues to Signal the Beginning and End of Class Periods*

Using visual and auditory cues, such as bells or announcements, to signal the beginning and end of class periods can help maintain structure and consistency throughout the school day. These cues remind students and staff to transition between classes and ensure everyone knows the current schedule. Schools can accommodate students with different learning styles and needs by combining visual and auditory cues. At one school, the principal played music over the intercom, and students knew that when the music played, they had 20 seconds left to get to class. They knew they would be late if the music stopped before they arrived at class. In another school, the principal used Promethean boards as timers. In the grade-level hallways, students would see exactly how much time they had before the bell would ring.

7. _Encourage Punctuality by Consistently Enforcing Tardy Policies_

Punctuality is essential for maintaining a positive school culture and ensuring students receive the full benefit of their educational experience. By consistently enforcing tardy policies, schools can promote responsibility and accountability among students and minimize disruptions caused by late arrivals. Consistent enforcement also helps to create a fair and equitable environment, as all students are held to the same standards and expectations.

Items to Consider:

1. The choice between the block and traditional master scheduling depends on the school's specific goals, needs, and priorities, as both systems have advantages and disadvantages.

2. Implementing a chosen master schedule effectively requires thoughtful consideration of the school's unique characteristics and the ability to adapt lesson plans and instructional strategies accordingly.

3. The bell schedule should be designed to optimize the overall educational experience, minimizing disruptions and maximizing the potential for order and productivity throughout the school day.

Reflection Questions:

1. How can we ensure that our chosen master scheduling system best aligns with our school's goals, needs, and priorities, and what steps can we take to implement it effectively?

2. What strategies can teachers employ to adapt their lesson plans and instructional approaches to the chosen master scheduling system, maximizing its benefits and minimizing its challenges?

3. How can we regularly evaluate the effectiveness of our master and bell schedules and make necessary adjustments to continue optimizing the learning environment for students and staff?

CHAPTER THREE:

KNOW THE STRUCTURE OF YOUR SCHOOL BUILDING

The structure of your school building plays a significant role in shaping the overall school experience for students and staff. A thoughtfully designed, well-organized school building can enhance learning, foster a positive environment, and promote safety and orderliness. In chapter three, "Know the Structure of Your School Building," we will delve into the various components that contribute to an efficient and conducive school structure and discuss the importance of each element. From designating specific areas for different activities to implementing effective traffic flow systems, we will examine the key aspects contributing to a well-rounded educational experience. We will also explore the importance of clear signage, staff supervision during high-traffic times, and marking exits, entrances, and emergency routes to ensure a safe and secure environment. By understanding these components, school administrators, teachers, and support staff can create a school building that facilitates academic success and nurtures students' social-emotional well-being.

1. *Designate Specific Areas for Different Activities*

Dedicated spaces for various activities allow students to focus on the task at hand and engage in their learning effectively. Quiet study zones offer students a calm and peaceful environment to concentrate on their assignments or catch up on their reading. Collaborative spaces encourage group work, problem-solving, and interactive learning. Recreational areas allow students to unwind, socialize, and participate in extracurricular activities. These designated spaces contribute to a well-rounded educational experience. Most schools have school libraries or media centers. Collaborating with your school Librarian and deciding how this space will be utilized is essential. Depending on its structure, this can be an area for quiet zones and collaborative learning. If your school has computer labs, there must be a process for how and when they will be used. Some schools now have reset or recharge rooms. Principals and counselors should develop expectations centered around the reset room's purpose and create clear procedures for how that room is to be utilized.

2. *Create Visible and Marked Signage*

Visible and marked signage helps students, staff, and visitors navigate the school building more efficiently. Clear signage reduces confusion, saves time, and promotes a sense of order within the school. Moreover, it contributes to the overall safety and security of the school community by directing people to appropriate areas and facilities.

3. *Implement an Effective Traffic Flow System*

A well-designed traffic flow system is essential for minimizing conges-tion and promoting orderly movement throughout the school building. Schools can ensure smooth transitions between classes and reduce the likelihood of bottlenecks or overcrowding by strategically placing en-trances, exits, staircases, and corridors. This system helps students ar-rive on time for their classes and reduces the risk of accidents and incidents in high-traffic areas. During the years of navigating the pan-demic, most schools used a one-way traffic system in specific hallways to reduce social distancing. Some schools have continued those proto-cols because it has led to a better-managed school building.

4. *Assign Staff to Monitor Problematic Areas During High-Traffic Times*

Supervision is a critical aspect of maintaining a safe and orderly school environment. Schools can deter misbehavior, resolve conflicts, and ad-dress safety concerns by assigning staff to monitor high-traffic areas during peak times. This initiative-taking approach helps maintain a pos-itive atmosphere, allowing students and staff to focus on their academic and professional responsibilities. I will address staff supervision more in chapter five.

5. *Mark Exits, Entrances, and Emergency Routes*

Safety should always be a top priority in any school environment. Marked exits, entrances, and emergency routes are vital for ensuring the well-being of students and staff in case of emergencies or evacuations.

Regularly reviewing and updating these markings and providing training on emergency procedures can help the school community respond effectively during critical situations.

Throughout chapter three, "Know the Structure of Your School Building," we have examined the vital role a well-organized and thoughtfully designed school building plays in creating a conducive learning environment. We explored the importance of designating specific areas for different activities, implementing effective traffic flow systems, and providing clear signage to ensure a smooth and efficient school experience.

We also discussed the necessity of staff supervision during high-traffic times and the marking of exits, entrances, and emergency routes to maintain a safe and secure environment. By understanding and implementing these essential components, school administrators, teachers, and support staff can work together to create a school building that fosters academic success and nurtures students' social-emotional well-being.

As we move forward in our quest to build a positive school environment, it is crucial to remember that the structure of the school building is a foundational aspect that influences every part of the educational experience. By prioritizing these elements, we can facilitate a well-rounded educational journey, ensuring our students have the necessary tools and resources to bloom in their academic pursuits and beyond.

Items to Consider:

1. Collaborating with the school librarian and other staff to optimize common spaces, such as libraries, media centers, and computer labs, is essential.

2. The potential benefits of maintaining pandemic-era traffic flow protocols, such as one-way hallways, are to reduce congestion and promote an orderly school environment.

3. Regularly reviewing and updating emergency routes and procedures, as well as providing training for students and staff, to ensure preparedness in case of emergencies or evacuations.

Reflection Questions:

1. How can we adapt the existing structure of our school building to designate spaces for different activities better and improve the overall learning experience?

2. What measures can we take to improve the traffic flow system within our school to minimize congestion and promote an orderly environment?

3. How can we better involve students, staff, and the school community in enhancing the school building's structure and organization, ensuring a more efficient and conducive learning environment?

Chapter Four:

Maximize Your Resources

Creating a positive school environment requires well-organized spaces, thoughtful design, and efficient use of available resources. This chapter will explore strategies for maximizing your school's resources to create a supportive and nurturing environment for students and staff. By understanding and implementing these strategies, school administrators, teachers, and support staff can work together to optimize their resources and provide the best educational experience.

1. *Utilize Staff Not in Classrooms for Additional Supervision and Support During Peak Times*

Non-classroom staff, such as administrative assistants, paraprofessionals, and even custodial staff, can be valuable resources during high-traffic times in the school building. By leveraging their assistance, schools can ensure that common areas, hallways, and other busy locations are adequately supervised, reducing the risk of misbehavior and enhancing overall school safety. For example, staff not involved in direct instruction can be strategically placed to monitor student movement and behavior during lunchtime or before and after school.

2. *Equip Staff with Walkie-Talkies for Efficient Communication*

Effective communication is essential for the smooth operation of a school building. Equipping staff members with walkie-talkies enables real-time communication and rapid response to issues. This can be particularly helpful during emergencies or when coordinating significant school events. For instance, if a student requires immediate assistance or a maintenance issue arises, staff can quickly relay the information using walkie-talkies, ensuring that appropriate personnel promptly address the situation. Deciding who will receive the walkie-talkies is necessary because there may be a limited supply. My life-skills teacher and my behavior support room teacher needed walkie-talkies because of the student population they served. My counselors and social workers had walkie-talkies because of the nature of their positions and the need to respond to student crises immediately. My school nurse needed a walkie-talkie to address emergency needs simultaneously, as we had many high-risk medical students.

3. *Establish Clear Communication Protocols Using Walkie-Talkies and Other Tools*

To maximize the effectiveness of walkie-talkies and other communication tools, it's essential to establish clear protocols for their use. This might include designating specific channels for different purposes, assigning call signs for individual staff members, and training staff to communicate succinctly and professionally. Walkie-talkies were only for quick communication items, not long conversations. Examples of some of the communications are, "Mr. Nunley, what is your location?" and "Mr. Nunley, I need assistance in room 313." We also did not use students' full names; we typically used student initials. We discussed with the team that regardless of the concern, everyone needed to speak calmly while using the walkie-talkies. We also focused on caring for the walkie-talkies and keeping them charged daily. Depending on the brand and its capabilities, some can cost up to $400 or more. Schools do not have unlimited resources, so ensuring they last is critical. These protocols will help keep an organized and efficient communication system that minimizes disruptions and enhances overall school operations.

4. *Use Bulletin Boards and Digital Displays to Share Important Information and Celebrate Student Achievements*

Bulletin boards and digital displays can be powerful tools for sharing essential information, celebrating student achievements, and promoting community within the school. Schools can keep students, staff, and visitors informed and engaged by regularly updating these displays with relevant content, such as upcoming events, student work samples, and positive news stories. For example, a school might display a monthly calendar of events on a digital screen in the main lobby or display student artwork on a bulletin board near the art classroom.

5. _Monitor Security Cameras to Identify Problem Areas and Address Issues Proactively_

Many schools are equipped with security cameras that can be a valuable resource for finding problem areas and addressing potential issues before they escalate. Regularly reviewing security footage can help administrators and staff spot patterns of misbehavior, unauthorized access, or other safety concerns. Schools can proactively address these issues and keep a safe and orderly environment. Typically, only administrators have access to security cameras. My administrative team would get training every year on all the features. Each team member had designated areas that they would keep up on their screen throughout the day. We knew these areas needed to be consistently monitored even when not in the hallway. When the cameras were installed, we worked with the district police officers and technology team to suggest the best possible locations. We also identified blind spots in our building so that we could always supervise those areas when individuals were available.

6. _Collaborate with Social Workers, Counselors, and Resource Officers to Address Students' Needs_

A successful school environment addresses academic needs and students' social-emotional well-being. Collaborating with social workers, counselors, and resource officers can help identify and address the unique needs of individual students. For example, counselors can provide targeted support for students experiencing personal challenges, while resource officers can collaborate with administrators to create a safe and secure learning environment. By leveraging the expertise of these professionals, schools can create a comprehensive support system that promotes student success and well-being. Counselors and social workers usually have a great pulse on what is happening in your school building. I held weekly meetings with them that covered a wide range of topics. We discussed the targeted needs they were addressing with the group and individual counseling sessions. Our counselors and social workers had a monthly event calendar for student activities. A section of our meeting was devoted to what was happening in the building. This is where I would learn the gossip happening in school and on social media. This information is robust because it allows you to avoid potential problems.

In conclusion, chapter four highlights the importance of efficiently using all available resources to create a positive and inclusive school environment. From utilizing non-classroom staff during peak times to effectively communicating through walkie-talkies and digital displays, these strategies demonstrate how schools can optimize resources to benefit students and staff. Moreover, schools can proactively address potential issues and support students' unique needs by monitoring security cameras and collaborating with various professionals, such as social workers, counselors, and resource officers. School administrators, teachers, and support staff can foster a supportive, safe, and nurturing environment that sets the foundation for a successful educational experience through understanding and implementing these approaches.

Items to Consider:

1. The importance of training staff in effectively using walkie-talkies and other communication tools to maintain organized and efficient communication systems.

2. Regularly updating bulletin boards and digital displays with relevant content to keep students, staff, and visitors informed and engaged while celebrating student achievements.

3. Identifying and addressing blind spots in school security camera coverage to ensure continuous monitoring and proactive supervision in all areas of the building.

Reflection Questions:

1. How can we better utilize non-classroom staff to support supervision and school safety during peak times?

2. What strategies can we implement to improve communication among staff members and ensure rapid response to situations as they arise?

3. How can we strengthen collaboration between school administrators, teachers, social workers, counselors, and resource officers to create a more comprehensive student support system?

STAFF SUPERVISION SCHEDULE

A successful and positive school environment relies heavily on the supervision administrators, teachers, and staff provide. A comprehensive supervision schedule is critical to creating a safe and orderly school setting. Chapter Five will discuss the importance of a staff supervision schedule, focusing on key elements such as creating a rotating schedule, ensuring adequate supervision during critical times, training staff to recognize and address potential behavioral issues, and providing clear expectations and guidelines for staff when supervising students.

1. *Create a Rotating Schedule for Administrators, Teachers, and Staff to Supervise High-Traffic Areas*

A rotating schedule ensures that high-traffic areas in the school, such as hallways, cafeterias, and playgrounds, are consistently monitored by staff. This schedule allows administrators, teachers, and staff to share supervision responsibilities and maintain a presence in these areas, which can deter misbehavior and promote safety and order. For example, a school might assign teachers to monitor hallways during class transitions while administrators supervise the cafeteria during lunch. The schedule should be organized and communicated clearly, making it easy for staff to understand their assigned locations and times. This is also where, from chapter four, monitoring blind spots, and, from chapter three, knowing the structure of your building is vital. Strategic staff placement in high-priority areas can do more to avoid issues than almost any other element. As principal, my school had the "five before and five after" rule for radio carriers that were not assigned to a classroom. Radio carriers were expected to be in their designated hallway location five minutes before the bell and five minutes after the bell during each transition period. There were, at times, emergencies where my team could not meet this requirement, but 90% of the time, we all did. This strategy served several purposes for us.

i.   Getting in the hallway early allowed us to control the traffic flow and immediately stopped kids from running in the hallway.

ii. Staying in the hallway five minutes after the bell allowed us to catch those tardy students lingering in the hallways.

iii. We could conduct bathroom sweeps to ensure students were not hiding in the stalls.

iv. The teachers saw us, and that assisted them in feeling supported and knowing that we were in the fight with them.

v.   Teachers would take this opportunity to express their concerns about a kid. Instead of writing a referral and sending them to the office, we could immediately meet with the kid and address the issue.

vi. You get to see the students more and interact with them.

One of the other strategies implemented was when the school lost an assistant principal, campus monitor, and resource officer. We were having trouble with students tearing down soap dispensers in our restrooms. When the staffing cuts occurred in my building, we needed more people and resources to monitor the restrooms adequately. My head custodian worked tirelessly to keep those restrooms clean and the soap dispensers available. It was also a cost to the school to keep replacing them. My head custodian and I created a rotational schedule where he would perform light clean-up in the restrooms throughout the day. On some days, he would do his restroom check on the odd periods one, three, five, and seven, and on other days he would complete them during the even periods two, four, six, and eight. First, the cleanliness of the restrooms immediately got better in the school. Second, we discovered who was tearing down the soap dispensers because we could narrow down the period and then utilize our school cameras to see who entered the restroom. Finally, after losing several key positions, it gave me another set of adult eyes to supervise the building.

2. *Ensure Adequate Supervision During Arrival, and Dismissal Times*

Arrival and dismissal times are often chaotic and require additional supervision to maintain order and safety. By assigning staff to these critical times, schools can minimize confusion, reduce the risk of accidents, and create a more structured environment for students. For instance, staff members can be stationed at key entry and exit points during arrival and dismissal times to monitor student movement. Ensuring adequate supervision during arrival and dismissal times is crucial for several school-specific reasons:

a. Traffic Control and Safety: During arrival and dismissal times, there is usually a significant increase in vehicle traffic as parents drop off and pick up their children. Staff members can help direct traffic, ensuring that vehicles follow appropriate routes and students enter or exit cars safely. This reduces the risk of accidents and creates a more structured environment for everyone.

b. Monitoring Unauthorized Visitors: Adequate supervision at entry and exit points allows staff to identify unauthorized individuals attempting to enter the school premises. This added layer of security helps maintain a safe environment for students and staff.

c. Preventing Bullying and Conflicts: Arrival and dismissal times can be moments when students may be more susceptible to bullying or conflicts. Staff presence and supervision can deter negative behaviors and enable staff to intervene promptly if any issues arise.

d. Attendance and Punctuality: Staff assigned to arrival times can help ensure students arrive on time and encourage punctuality.

They can also quickly identify students who may be habitually late, enabling the school to address any underlying issues causing tardiness.

e. Smooth Transition to After-School Activities: For students participating in after-school activities, adequate supervision during dismissal times can ensure they transition smoothly to their respective programs. Staff can provide directions, answer questions, and ensure students are accounted for.

f. Parent Communication: Staff assigned to arrival and dismissal times can serve as a point of contact for parents, addressing any concerns or questions. This can help foster open communication between the school and parents, leading to a stronger sense of community and partnership.

g. Lost and Found Items: Students may accidentally leave behind personal belongings during arrival and dismissal times. Adequate supervision allows staff to collect and secure lost items, helping to reunite them with their owners.

By ensuring proper supervision during arrival and dismissal times, schools can create a safer, more structured environment that supports the well-being and success of their students.

3. _Train Staff to Recognize and Address Potential Behavioral Issues Before They Escalate_

Adequate supervision is not just about being present; staff must also be equipped to recognize and address potential behavioral issues before they escalate. Training staff on identifying warning signs of conflict, understanding age-appropriate behaviors, and employing de-escalation techniques can empower them to intervene proactively and maintain a positive school environment. For example, staff can be trained to recognize verbal and non-verbal cues that suggest a student may be agitated and then use calming techniques or refer the student to a counselor or administrator for additional support.

My team always paid close attention to student grouping and moved immediately to separate them to keep traffic moving. Very few positive things I have experienced occur when students group in a specific area in the hallway. Moving toward those areas and asking students to keep moving toward class was an expectation for my team. As students moved outside toward buses, supervision became more challenging. Before the year, we developed a bus supervision schedule and plan. Staff members were placed in strategic areas so that we could cover the entire area. Our goal was to dismiss the school buses six minutes after dismissal. At the five-minute mark, our bus drivers honked their horns to let everyone know they had one minute to go. There were times when students were left at the school and later had to contact parents for a ride, but usually, this only occurred a couple of times as students quickly learned the expectation. Below is a sample of our AM/PM bus procedures plan.

AM BUS PROCEDURES FOR ENTRY INTO THE BUILDING:

- *When buses arrive at the building, they will park in their designated slot number. **Slot numbers 19-28 are part of Side A between doors 15 and 16. Slot numbers 29-40 are part of Side B between doors 16 and 17.***

- *We will release students from their buses by grade level. However, they will be released by odd slot numbers first and then by even slot numbers. This will allow for a decrease in the number of students entering the building at once.*

- *This year, we will allow 7th and 8th-grade students in bus slot numbers 19-28 to enter the building through Door 15.*

SIDE A BUS SLOTS:

*19, 20, 21, 22, 23, 24, 25, 26, 27, 28 **(Side A- Between Door 15 and 16)***

All 8th graders in these slots will enter through Door 15.
***First wave**-odd numbers, then even.*

All 7th graders in these slots will enter through Door 15.
***Second wave**-odd numbers then even.*

All 6th graders in these slots will enter through Door 15.
***Third wave**-odd numbers then even.*

SIDE B BUS SLOTS:

29, 30, 31, 32, 33, 34, 35, 36, 37, 38, 39, 40, *(Side B-Between Door 16 and Door 17)*

All 8th graders in these slots will enter through Door 19.
First wave-odd numbers, then even.

All 7th graders in these slots will enter through Door 17.
Second wave- odd numbers, then even.

All 6th graders in these slots will enter through Door 16.
Third wave- odd numbers, then even.

PM BUS PROCEDURES FOR EXITING THE BUILDING TO THE BUSES:

- **The PA announcement will dismiss our students.** *We will release our students by grade level and hallway within the grade level wings. Teachers are not to dismiss students on their own. Teachers should encourage students to get their belongings from their lockers and report immediately to the buses.*

- *Dismissal will be staggered by one minute. For example, 8th grade Side A will be dismissed first. Then 8th Grade Side B will be dismissed second. This will happen for each grade level.*

- *All Related Arts students will be dismissed after all the wings have been dismissed.*

- *All car riders will report to Door 3.*

- *Coaches and sponsors must have their athletes and students report directly to their designated after-school area.*

<u>Students will be dismissed over the PA by grade level in this order:</u>

<u>6th Grade Side A Teachers:</u>

<u>6th Grade Side B Teachers:</u>

<u>7th Grade Side A Teachers:</u>

<u>7th Grade Side B Teachers:</u>

<u>8th Grade Side A Teachers:</u>

<u>8th grade Side B teachers:</u>

The AM/PM, bus procedures plan played a crucial role in organizing the arrival and departure of students, ensuring a safe and efficient experience for everyone involved. The specific details in the plan were essential for several reasons.

First, the plan facilitated efficient and timely dismissal by setting a clear goal of dismissing buses within six minutes of the school day's end. This precision allowed students to reach home promptly and parents to coordinate their schedules accordingly.

Second, the plan prioritized safety through the staggered release of students by grade level and bus slot numbers, reducing congestion and overcrowding during arrival and departure. This approach minimized the likelihood of accidents or altercations, contributing to a safer environment for students and staff.

Third, the plan established clear expectations for punctuality and responsibility, with reminders like the bus horn honking at the five-minute mark. This system encouraged students to be mindful of their schedules and board buses promptly.

Furthermore, the strategic placement of staff members ensured thorough supervision and guidance during arrival and departure, maintaining order and discipline among students. The allocation of specific doors and bus slots streamlined entry and exit, reducing confusion and preventing delays.

The plan also incorporated a PA announcement system to communicate dismissal orders, ensuring that every student knew the procedures and could follow them accordingly.

Finally, it accounted for students participating in after-school activities, providing clear instructions for reporting to designated areas.

In conclusion, the detailed AM/PM bus procedures plan was vital for the safe, efficient, and orderly organization of arrival and departure. The specific details were crucial in minimizing delays, confusion, and safety concerns, contributing to a more positive school environment.

4. *Provide Clear Expectations and Guidelines for Staff When Supervising Students*

Establishing clear expectations and guidelines for staff when supervising students is essential for maintaining consistency and promoting a positive school culture. These guidelines should outline the roles and responsibilities of staff during supervision, including how to address misbehavior, support students in need, and communicate effectively with colleagues. By providing staff with a clear understanding of their responsibilities during supervision, schools can foster a sense of accountability and professionalism, ensuring that every member of the school community is working towards a shared goal of creating a safe and supportive environment for students.

5. *Supporting Substitute Teachers*

Substitute teachers are vital in maintaining continuity and stability when the regular teacher is absent. To ensure a smooth and effective transition, the school staff must provide support and guidance for the substitute teacher regarding the supervision schedule. The following steps can be taken to assist substitute teachers in navigating and fulfilling their supervision responsibilities:

a. Provide a Detailed Supervision Schedule: Share the existing supervision schedule with the substitute teacher, including specific times, locations, and responsibilities. This will allow the substitute to understand their role in maintaining a safe and orderly school environment, enabling them to effectively supervise students during their time at the school.

b. Assign a Point of Contact: Designate a staff member as a substitute teacher's point of contact. This person can provide guidance, answer questions, and address the substitute's concerns about their supervision responsibilities. This support helps the substitute feel more confident and integrated into the school community.

c. Offer Training and Resources: Provide the substitute teacher with training materials and resources on recognizing and addressing potential behavioral issues and any school-specific policies and procedures related to student supervision. This information will equip the substitute with the necessary tools to maintain a safe and positive learning environment.

d. Communicate Expectations: Communicate the expectations and guidelines for student supervision to the substitute teacher, emphasizing the importance of their role in maintaining a safe and orderly school setting. The substitute teacher can be more confident and effective in supervision by understanding the expectations.

e. Encourage Collaboration and Communication: Encourage the substitute teacher to collaborate and communicate with other staff members, particularly those sharing supervision duties in high-traffic areas. This collaboration can help ensure a seamless transition and allow the substitute to better understand the school's culture and supervision practices.

f. Provide Feedback and Support: Regularly check in with the substitute teacher to provide feedback on their supervision efforts and address any challenges they may face. This ongoing support can help the substitutes improve their skills and adapt to the school environment more effectively.

Schools can maintain a safe and positive learning environment by supporting substitute teachers with a supervision schedule, even when regular staff members are absent. Providing clear guidance, training, and resources for substitute teachers can help them fulfill their supervision responsibilities effectively, ensuring that students continue to receive the support they need to succeed.

In conclusion, chapter five emphasizes the importance of a well-designed and comprehensive staff supervision schedule in creating a positive school environment. By implementing a rotating schedule, ensuring adequate supervision during critical times, training staff to recognize and address potential behavioral issues, and providing clear expectations and guidelines, schools can maintain a safe and orderly setting for students to learn and grow. Establishing a solid supervision system helps to foster a sense of community and shared responsibility, allowing staff and students to focus on achieving academic success and personal growth.

Items to Consider:

1. Create an effective rotating schedule that equally distributes supervision responsibilities among administrators, teachers, and staff.

2. Training staff in conflict resolution, de-escalation techniques, and understanding age-appropriate behaviors to manage potential issues better is essential.

3. Clear expectations and guidelines for staff during supervision are needed to promote consistency and professionalism.

Reflection Questions:

1. How can a school adapt its staff supervision schedule to address unique challenges, such as limited resources or staffing cuts?

2. How can schools improve communication among staff members to ensure a seamless supervision experience and enhance overall school safety?

3. How can schools involve parents, students, and the broader community in creating a safe and supportive environment through effective supervision practices?

CHAPTER SIX

SCHOOL-WIDE CLASSROOM EXPECTATIONS

A healthy learning environment relies on consistently implementing clear and well-defined expectations for behavior and routines. Establishing school-wide classroom expectations ensures that students understand what is required of them, regardless of their classroom. This chapter will discuss the importance of school-wide classroom expectations, expanding each element with specific school-related examples.

1. *Develop Clear and Consistent Expectations for Behavior and Routines in All Classrooms: Creating* clear and consistent classroom expectations promotes unity and understanding among students and staff. These expectations may include behavior, participation, organization rules, and routines for transitioning between activities or managing materials. For example, a school might rule that all students raise their hands to ask questions or contribute to discussions, ensuring every student has an equal opportunity to participate without interruption.

2. *Train Teachers to Implement and Enforce These Expectations Effectively:* To ensure that school-wide classroom expectations are consistently applied, it is essential to provide training and support for teachers. Professional development sessions, workshops, and ongoing coaching can help teachers implement and enforce these classroom expectations effectively. For instance, a school might offer a workshop on positive behavior management strategies to help teachers encourage and reinforce appropriate student conduct.

3. *Communicate Expectations to Students and Parents Through Multiple Channels:* For school-wide classroom expectations to be effective, they must be communicated to students and their families. This communication can take various forms, including parent-teacher conferences, newsletters, websites, and social media. By sharing expectations through multiple channels, schools can ensure that all members of the school community understand what is expected of students. For example, a school might create a poster outlining its behavior expectations, display it in every classroom, and provide a digital version for parents to access online.

4. *Communicate These Expectations and the Consequences of Not Following Them:* In addition to outlining expectations, it is essential to establish and communicate the consequences of not adhering to them. Students and parents can better understand the importance of compliance by clearly explaining the potential outcomes of not following school-wide classroom expectations. The consequences should be fair, consistent, and appropriate for the infraction, ranging from verbal reminders to more significant interventions, such

as parent meetings or disciplinary action. For example, a school might implement a system where students receive a verbal warning for a first-time infraction, a written notice, parent contact, and further consequences for repeated violations.

Here is an example of what we used as our school-wide classroom expectations.

School-Wide Classroom Expectations and Discipline Policy

Be Ready	Be Respectful	Be Responsible	Be Awesome
Be in your assigned seat or teacher-designated area when the bell rings, or you will need a tardy pass to enter class.	Treat your peers, teachers, and guests to our room respectfully and courteously.	Give your best effort on all assignments, activities, and assessments.	Think for yourself!
Come to class each day with all your materials. You will need paper, pens, book(s), a device, and any work due.	Blurting out, interruptions, and rudeness will not be tolerated. No profanity or "sound-alike" words.	DO YOUR WORK! No copying homework or plagiarizing.	Think Deeply!
Be attentive! No sleeping, slouching, or laying your head down.	Raise your hand and wait to be acknowledged.	You are responsible for getting any missed notes, assignments, and assessments given during your absence and submitting all assignments by the assigned due date.	Take risks and work hard!
Actively participate in group work, discussions, and classroom activities.	Respect our space by not eating candy, chewing gum, or selling candy or food in the classroom. During class, there is no grooming (combing/brushing hair, putting on lotion, perfume/ cologne, etc.).	Using technology at inappropriate times is rude, and per school policy, phones are to remain in your locker during the school day—no phones in the classroom. Remember, you control your technology; it shouldn't control you.	Practice P.A.W.S.! Practice Respect Accept Responsibility Work Together Safety Matters .

In my first year as principal, I noticed that the school needed more alignment regarding our classroom expectations. Suppose you have spent considerable time in education. In that case, you have heard students complain about inconsistencies in the process, such as, in Mrs. Jones's room, I am allowed to have my cell phone out, so I do not understand why it is a problem in Mr. Nunley's classroom. The students are right; the expectation is not consistent. I had a grade-level team that year, and I heard the students call the teachers petty. Petty in teenage language means "making a big deal out of a minor issue." What was different is that it did not matter about the classroom or the teacher; the expectation was the same. If one teacher told you about no earbuds in class, all the teachers expected it. This team did not mess around. Getting the students to conform took work, but eventually, they met the expectation. Qualitatively and then quantitively, the evidence was clear that I was dealing with more issues with the other teams because they were not as consistent as a unit. That is when I determined we must have school-wide classroom expectations and work together to make them clear to all students. We added a consistent training schedule throughout the year centered around those school-wide classroom expectations, and I guess you can argue that my entire school building was petty. More importantly, we had students engaged, learning was happening in classrooms, and students were not spending time in the office with me.

Items to Consider:

1. The process of developing and refining school-wide classroom expectations, including how to gather input from teachers, students, and parents.

2. The methods and resources used to train teachers to consistently implement and enforce these expectations.

3. The approaches to communicating expectations and consequences to students and parents ensure that all stakeholders are informed and engaged.

Reflection Questions:

1. How can schools ensure that the development and implementation of schoolwide classroom expectations are an inclusive and collaborative process involving teachers, students, and parents?

2. What strategies can schools employ to continuously evaluate the effectiveness of their schoolwide classroom expectations and make necessary adjustments?

3. How can schools balance the need for consistency in expectations and consequences with addressing individual student needs and circumstances?

CHAPTER SEVEN

CAFETERIA PLAN

A well-organized and effectively managed cafeteria is critical in creating a positive school environment, as it is an essential space where students gather, socialize, and recharge. A comprehensive cafeteria plan ensures that mealtimes are structured, safe, and conducive to fostering a sense of community among students. This chapter will discuss the critical elements of a successful cafeteria plan and provide school-related examples to illustrate their significance.

I understand the challenge of managing the cafeteria for schools. I recall my first year as an assistant principal, and I oversaw the 6th-grade lunch. Our 6th-grade class had about 325 students, which is significant for a middle school grade level. Fifth-grade students at the elementary schools had smaller lunch periods and traditionally ate lunch with their classmates. This experience in the middle school cafeteria was as new to them as it was to me. Teachers would bring their class down to the cafeteria and scatter away quickly, as if they knew what would happen. The students entered the cafeteria and sat at the table with their teacher's name on it, which escorted them to that cafeteria. I will tell you in a moment why that's a bad idea in middle school.

The first thing I noticed was students arguing and trying to sit on top of each other so they could sit next to a specific person. Then I saw that the number of students in a class did not match the number of seats at the table. This caused students to need to find other seats at other tables. Once everyone was seated, I was then able to notice how loud it was in that cafeteria. So, you do the things they tell you in administrative school; wait, they do not tell you anything about this in administrative school, so you do what the other assistant principal did with the seventh graders. I did a countdown on the microphone and waved my hand to get their attention. I clapped it up and then got loud on the microphone. None of those are long-term strategies, by the way, but it eventually worked. As I explained the lunch process, and school rules in the cafeteria and communicated what was on the lunch menu, I noticed that we only had about 25 minutes to go before the next group of students was scheduled to eat. So now I am rushing to get 6th-grade students through the lunch line that have never had this many choices and do not know their ID numbers. Let's say it was a mess, and we were about 30 minutes late.

Now back to the students sitting at the table by the teacher that brought them down to the cafeteria. The teacher that picks them up differs from the teacher that brings them down to the cafeteria. Students, teachers, and I were confused, and I was sure I was quitting or getting fired. I did not leave, and the principal was willing to be patient, as I learned. I slowly but surely began to get some management over the situation.

It took at least one semester before I felt okay. Those lessons manifested in my mind forever, so I would never allow that experience to occur again. So, collaborating with my team, we developed some guidelines that worked for our cafeteria environment.

Student behavior expectations:

Table Procedures –
- Students will enter quietly and sit at their assigned table (fourth, fifth, and sixth-period teachers).
- Students quietly will listen to announcements for the day and wait to be released to talk by the administrator on duty.
- Students will keep their hands and feet to themselves and will remain seated once they are at the assigned lunch table.
- Students will clean their space before leaving, putting all food and paper in the trash cans.

Lunch Line Procedures –
- Students will report to the lunch line when their table is called. Students facing the right wall of the cafeteria will walk to their left, while students facing the left wall will walk to their right and will meet in the center aisle to walk into the serving area.
- Students will receive their food and say "thank you" to the cafeteria staff. They will then go through a checkout line where they must scan their student ID.
- Students will not be allowed to re-enter the serving area after checking out, so they need to get everything, including utensils, napkins, and water, the first time through.

- Students will walk back down the center aisle to their designated table and seat.

Exiting Procedures –

- Once their area is clean, students will be dismissed by the table to their teachers.
- Students should not stand or leave the cafeteria until the administrator on duty has dismissed them.
- Trash cans will be circulating in the cafeteria, and all trash should be disposed of appropriately.
- Students will form a straight line, using hallway procedures to exit the cafeteria.

<u>Supervision Responsibilities:</u>

- Teachers will deliver and pick up students from the cafeteria at the appointed time.
- Teachers, while on duty, will circulate through assigned areas in the cafeteria, monitor student behavior, and aid in maintaining the cleanliness of the cafeteria.
- Teachers will ensure that tables are clean before students are dismissed from the cafeteria.

<u>Restroom Use:</u>

- The expectation is that students use the bathroom before arriving at lunch. If a student has an emergency and needs to use the bathroom, use your discretion.
- Students (three at a time) will be allowed to use the restrooms outside the auditorium during lunch if they submit their student

ID. IDs will be returned to students when they return from the restroom.

- Please remind students to return to the cafeteria as quickly as possible.

Correcting Misbehavior:

When students do not follow cafeteria procedures, calmly and consistently implement a mild, appropriate consequence. Positive practice and a verbal reminder should be consistently used for at least the first two weeks before using other consequences unless the behavior is severe and warrants attention from the administrator on duty.

1. Positive practice – have the student try again.

2. Verbal reminder

3. Misbehavior in line – Have the student go to the end of the line.

4. Misbehavior at a table if verbal reminders do not correct –

    a. Assigned seating.

    b. Lunch detention

5. Physically dangerous behavior or severe defiance should be taken to the administrator on duty immediately.

Below is a summary of what is needed for an effectively run cafeteria.

1. _Ensure Adequate Supervision and Enforce Behavioral Expectations During Mealtimes:_ Maintaining a safe and orderly cafeteria requires proper supervision from school staff during mealtimes. Schools can ensure students follow established rules and behavioral expectations by assigning teachers, administrators, or support staff to monitor the cafeteria. Supervisors can promptly address conflicts or misbehavior, promoting a positive atmosphere in the cafeteria. For example, a school may create a rotating schedule for staff members to supervise the cafeteria, ensuring that every staff member can oversee this responsibility and that all staff members are familiar with the cafeteria's routines and expectations.

2. _Establish Clear Rules and Procedures for the Cafeteria:_ Developing and implementing clear rules and procedures for the cafeteria is essential to maintaining order and creating a pleasant dining experience for students. These rules may include designated seating areas for different grade levels or classes, proper food disposal, and acceptable noise levels. By outlining and consistently enforcing these expectations, schools can minimize confusion and create a more enjoyable environment for students. For instance, a school might assign each grade level a specific seating area in the cafeteria, reducing the likelihood of overcrowding and helping students find their peers more easily. Additionally, schools may establish guidelines for proper food disposal, ensuring that students clean up after themselves and contribute to a tidy cafeteria.

3. *<u>Encourage Students to Take Responsibility for Maintaining a Clean and Orderly Eating Environment</u>:* Fostering a sense of responsibility among students is crucial for maintaining a clean and orderly cafeteria. Schools can promote this by assigning specific tasks to students, such as wiping down tables, disposing of trash, or returning trays to designated areas. By involving students in the upkeep of the cafeteria, schools can instill a sense of pride and ownership in the shared space. For example, a school may implement a rotating system where each class cleans the cafeteria after lunch. This teaches students valuable life skills and helps reduce the burden on the custodial staff.

In conclusion, a well-planned cafeteria strategy is vital for creating a positive school environment that supports students' social and emotional well-being. Schools can create a safe, orderly, and pleasant space for students to relax, socialize, and refuel during mealtimes by ensuring adequate supervision, establishing clear rules and procedures, and encouraging students to take responsibility for their eating environment.

Items to Consider:

1. Consistency in Supervision: Ensure all staff members who supervise the cafeteria are familiar with the routines and expectations. Consider creating a rotating schedule for staff members to manage the cafeteria to maintain consistency.

2. Communication of Rules and Procedures: Effectively communicate the cafeteria rules and procedures to students, parents, and

staff. Regular reminders and reinforcement of these expectations can help maintain a pleasant dining environment.

3. Customization to School Needs: Consider the unique needs and characteristics of the student population and school environment when designing a cafeteria plan. Tailor the plan to address specific challenges or requirements in your school setting.

Reflection Questions:

1. How can the school ensure all staff members are familiar with and consistently enforce the cafeteria rules and procedures?

2. What strategies can be implemented to effectively communicate the cafeteria expectations to students, parents, and staff?

3. How can the school involve students in maintaining a clean and orderly cafeteria, and what benefits can be gained from their involvement?

Chapter Eight:

Cell Phone Plan

Cell phones have become an integral part of our daily lives in today's digital age. While they offer numerous benefits, their presence in schools can pose challenges, including distractions and potential misuse. Schools must establish an effective cell phone plan to promote a focused and respectful learning environment. This chapter will discuss the critical elements of a successful cell phone plan and provide specific school-related examples.

When I ask teachers what one of their biggest concerns is, the cell phone issue is easily in the top three. Cell phones bring multiple distractions, such as texting in class, social media, and parents calling their children during school. Some schools and teachers allow students to use them for in-class assignments. In high school, cell phones, at times, are the primary device they utilize. Below are several components schools need to consider.

1. *Establish a Clear and Consistent Cell Phone Policy for Students During the School Day*: A well-defined cell phone policy is crucial for setting expectations and maintaining an orderly school environment. This policy should outline when and where students are allowed to use their phones and any restrictions on usage during specific times, such as during class, in the hallways, or at lunch. For example, a school might implement a policy that permits cell phone use only during breaks and lunch, or it may require students to keep their phones silenced and stored in their lockers during the school day.

2. *Communicate the Policy to Students, Parents, and Staff*: To ensure that all stakeholders understand and adhere to the cell phone policy, it is vital to communicate the rules clearly and consistently. This might involve discussing the policy during parent-teacher conferences, posting the guidelines on the school website, and reviewing the rules during student assemblies. Additionally, teachers should be trained to enforce the policy consistently, ensuring that all students are treated fairly and held accountable for their actions.

3. *Consistently Enforce Consequences for Students Who Violate the Cellphone Policy*: To maintain a focused learning environment, schools must consistently enforce consequences for students who violate the cell phone policy. These consequences should be clearly defined and communicated to students and parents. For instance, a school may implement a three-strike system, where the first violation results in a warning, the second violation requires the student to surrender their phone to the office for the remainder of the day, and the third violation leads to a parent-teacher conference and potential loss of

cell phone privileges. Below is an example of a policy I used as a principal with four steps.

FOUR-STEP PROCESS TO MANAGE CELL PHONES/EARBUDS OR ANY ELECTRONIC DEVICE!

STEP ONE) In a non-confrontational way, remind students of the cell phone policy and allow them to put it in their locker. Avoid taking cell phones from students as we do not want to have any responsibility for them. Make a quick note that has the date and time of your conversation.

STEP TWO) If it is the second time they have their cell phone out, tell them again to put it away in their locker, and that you will need to communicate with their parents. When you communicate, please ask the parents for their assistance. Let them know you have had to ask them to put it away once already. Let the guardian know you want to avoid sending them to the office with a referral and need them to focus on class. You can communicate via phone or send an email.

STEP THREE) Student again has their cell phone in class after your phone call. Please send them to their locker to put it away and email your administrator overseeing the discipline. You do not need to get into any discussion with the student when they return from their locker. The administrator will determine how they will handle it after their conversation with the student. Please document the dates of the previous two steps in your email.

STEP FOUR) If the student has a cell phone in your class again, proceed immediately to a referral. Again, ask the student to put it away in their locker. Refrain from getting into any debate or conversation about the issue when the student returns to class. Turn in the referral at your earliest convenience. Move forward with **step four** for any other occurrences moving forward.

Notes) If a student refuses to put their cell phone in their locker at any stage, that is a failure to comply and an immediate referral to the administrator. Please work with the students to help them understand the importance of complying with your request.

Notes) Your responsibility in the hallways is to remind students that all electronic devices must be placed in their lockers. You do not need to follow students or aggressively confront them. Trust that your colleagues will do their part when the student arrives at their class. Only document occurrences in your classroom!

4. *Provide Alternatives for Students to Access Important Information and Resources:* Recognizing that students may need to access information and resources during the school day, schools should provide alternatives to using cell phones. This might involve designating computer labs or providing students with tablets during designated times. By offering these alternatives, schools can ensure students can access the necessary resources while maintaining a distraction-free learning environment. For example, a school may allow students to use the computer lab during lunch breaks to complete assignments or research or provide classroom tablets for group work during class time.

In conclusion, an effective cell phone plan is essential for maintaining a focused, respectful, and productive learning environment. By establishing a clear and consistent policy, communicating the rules to all stakeholders, enforcing consequences for policy violations, and providing alternatives for students to access essential resources, schools can successfully manage cell phone usage and ensure that students remain engaged and attentive during the school day.

Items to Consider:

1. Balancing the educational benefits of using technology in the classroom with the potential distractions and misuse of cell phones.

2. Determining the appropriate consequences for students who violate the cell phone policy, ensuring fairness and consistency in enforcement.

3. Addressing the digital divide among students who may need equal access to technology and ensuring that all students have access to necessary resources.

Reflection Questions:

1. How can educators integrate technology into the classroom to minimize distractions and misuse of cell phones while still promoting engagement and learning?

2. How can schools effectively involve parents in developing and enforcing cell phone policies, ensuring all stakeholders understand and support the rules?

3. How can schools provide equal access to technology and resources for all students, considering the varying levels of access to personal devices and technology at home?

CHAPTER NINE

REWARDS AND CONSEQUENCES

A well-balanced system of rewards and consequences is crucial for fostering a positive school environment, promoting good behavior, and ensuring students understand their actions' consequences. This chapter will discuss the importance of a reward system, outline the consequences of not meeting behavior expectations, and provide specific school examples.

1. *Implement a School-wide System for Acknowledging and Celebrating Positive Behavior:* Creating a positive learning environment involves recognizing and celebrating students' achievements and good behavior. A school-wide system for acknowledging positive behavior can motivate students to make better choices, contribute to a sense of community, and reinforce desired behaviors. Examples of reward systems include:

- "Student of the Month" awards, where teachers nominate students with exceptional behavior or academic achievement.

- Positive behavior points, which students can accumulate for exhibiting good behavior and later redeem for rewards such as special privileges or small prizes.

- Class or grade-level competitions, where classes or grades can earn points for positive behavior, and the winning group is rewarded with a special event or activity.

2. *Develop a Consistent and Fair System of Consequences for Students Who Do Not Meet Behavior Expectations:* While rewarding positive behavior is essential, it is equally important to establish a consistent and fair system of consequences for students who do not meet behavior expectations. This system should be communicated to students, parents, and staff and applied consistently across the school. Consequences should be proportional to the infraction and may include:

- Verbal warnings or reminders of the expected behavior

- Time-outs or temporary removal from the classroom

- Detention or loss of privileges

- Parent-teacher conferences

- Suspension or expulsion for severe or repeated offenses

3. *Involve Students and Parents in the Developing and Implementing Rewards and Consequences:* Involving students and parents in developing

and implementing rewards and consequences can help build a sense of ownership and collaboration within the school community. This process might include the following:

- Soliciting input from students and parents through surveys, focus groups, or school council meetings.

- Regularly reviewing and adjusting the reward and consequence systems based on feedback from the school community.

- Engaging parents in celebrating their child's achievements, such as inviting them to award ceremonies or sending home positive behavior notes.

In conclusion, establishing a system of rewards and consequences is essential for managing a school effectively. By implementing a school-wide strategy for acknowledging and celebrating positive behavior, developing a consistent and fair system of consequences, and involving students and parents, schools can promote a positive learning environment, encourage good behavior, and ensure that all students can succeed.

Items to Consider:

1. Identifying the most effective rewards and incentives to motivate students and encourage positive behavior while also being mindful of potential issues such as competition or unfairness.

2. Ensuring that consequences are applied consistently and fairly across the school to avoid enforcement disparities and promote a sense of fairness among students.

3. Evaluating the effectiveness of the reward and consequence systems in promoting positive behavior and addressing negative behavior and adjusting the methods based on feedback and data.

Reflection Questions:

1. How can schools balance rewarding positive behavior and addressing negative behavior to ensure all students can learn and grow in a supportive environment?

2. What strategies can be employed to ensure that students view negative behavior's consequences as fair and an opportunity for growth and learning rather than simply as punishment?

3. How can schools effectively involve students and parents in developing and implementing rewards and consequences, and what challenges might arise?

<hr>

CHAPTER TEN

RELATIONSHIPS WITH STUDENTS AND PARENTS

The relationships between students, parents, and school staff play a critical role in creating a positive school environment. Strong connections between these groups foster a sense of community, promote open communication, and contribute to the overall success of the students. This chapter will discuss the importance of nurturing relationships with students and parents and provide specific school examples. As important as it is to develop relationships with parents and establish open communication channels, parents do not dictate what happens in schools. Sometimes, the parents will have differing views on how the school has chosen to manage a situation. There may be policies that parents disagree about the school enforcing. They have a right to state their opinion, and schools should listen to their perspective. Principals manage schools, and teachers are the priority personnel resources assisting in that process. Yes, parents are taxpayers, but an entire organization is in place that decides policy to manage a school system. Educators must have years of schooling and recertifications throughout their careers to show they are qualified. School personnel must utilize that expertise and experience even when it may conflict with a parent's desires. Here are some examples of how schools can build successful relationships with students and parents.

1. *Foster Strong Relationships with Students and Parents through Regular Communication and Engagement Opportunities*: Regular communication with students and parents can help build trust, address concerns, and keep families informed about their child's progress. Examples of communication and engagement opportunities include:

   - Parent-teacher conferences, where parents and teachers can discuss a student's academic progress, behavior, and concerns.

   - Regular newsletters and email updates inform parents about school events, policies, and announcements.

   - Open house events, where parents can visit the school, meet teachers, and learn about classroom expectations and curriculum.

2. *Offer Opportunities for Parent Involvement in School Activities and Decision-Making*: Encouraging parents to be involved in school activities and decision-making processes can contribute to a sense of ownership and investment in the school community. Examples of parent involvement opportunities include:

   - Parent-teacher organizations offer parents a platform to collaborate with school staff and support school initiatives.

- School committees or councils, where parents can participate in making decisions related to school policies, budgets, and improvement plans.

- Volunteering opportunities include helping with school events, serving as chaperones on field trips, or assisting in the classroom.

3. _Provide Resources and Support for Families to Address Challenges at Home and Promote a Positive Home Environment_: Schools can play a crucial role in supporting families to overcome challenges and promote a positive home environment that contributes to student success. Examples of support and resources include:

- Parent workshops or seminars may cover effective communication, conflict resolution, or academic support strategies.

- Referrals to community resources, such as counseling services, tutoring programs, or financial assistance for needy families.

- Providing resources and materials for parents to support their child's learning and development at home.

4. _Encourage Open Communication between School Staff, Students, and Parents_: Open communication between school staff, students, and parents fosters trust, collaboration, and a sense of shared responsibility for student success. Schools can promote open communication by:

- Providing multiple channels for communication, such as email, phone calls, or face-to-face meetings.

- Encouraging students and parents to express their concerns, ask questions, and share feedback.

- Actively seeking input from students and parents on school policies, initiatives, and improvements.

5. _Build Trust and Rapport with Students by Showing Genuine Interest in Their Well-Being:_ When school staff shows genuine interest in students' well-being, it fosters trust, rapport, and a sense of belonging. Examples of building trust and rapport with students include:

- Taking time to listen and engage with students, whether in the classroom, during lunch, or at school events.

- Showing empathy and understanding when students face challenges or express concerns.

- Celebrating students' achievements and acknowledging their strengths and interests.

6. _Provide Regular Updates on School Policies, Events, and Student Progress:_ Keeping parents informed about school policies, events, and their child's progress helps maintain open communication and demonstrates the school's commitment to transparency. Regular updates can be shared through:

- Progress reports, report cards, or online portals that provide updates on a student's academic performance and behavior.

- School websites, social media, or email blasts that share information about upcoming events and important dates.

- School assemblies or parent meetings, where updates on school policies, initiatives, and successes are shared.

Strong relationships between students, parents, and staff are crucial to establishing a positive school environment. Schools can create an inclusive and supportive atmosphere that benefits all community members by focusing on regular communication, parent involvement, resource support, open communication, building trust and rapport, and providing updates on policies, events, and student progress. As we have seen throughout this chapter, nurturing these relationships requires a multifaceted approach that includes various strategies and initiatives. By implementing these strategies, schools can enhance academic performance and student engagement and create a powerful sense of community and belonging for everyone involved. Ultimately, the relationships between students, parents, and school staff form the foundation of a successful and thriving educational experience. By prioritizing these connections, schools can create an environment where students can grow, learn, and succeed.

Items to Consider:

1. The balance between welcoming parental involvement and ensuring educators maintain their authority and expertise in managing the school and making decisions.

2. The role of cultural sensitivity and understanding in nurturing relationships with diverse students and families, ensuring that communication and engagement strategies are inclusive and effective.

3. The potential challenges of managing communication and relationships with many students and families and identifying strategies for maintaining personal connections in a busy school environment.

Reflection Questions:

1. How can educators and school administrators prioritize relationship-building with students and parents while managing the many other demands of their roles?

2. What strategies can be implemented to ensure communication and engagement with parents and students is effective, timely, and accessible for all school community members?

3. How can schools support educators and staff in developing the skills and strategies to foster strong relationships with students and parents and constructively address potential conflicts or challenges?

In conclusion, the ten components outlined in this book are designed to provide educators with a comprehensive and practical approach to creating a positive school environment. By implementing these strategies, schools can foster a culture of inclusivity, respect, and belonging while managing a dynamic learning environment's daily operations and challenges. From creating a positive school culture to building strong relationships with students and parents, each component plays a vital role in shaping the overall school experience.

The practical processes in this book have been evaluated and refined over time, resulting in a proven framework for educators to apply in any school environment. This book goes beyond theory and provides actionable steps to implement immediately, leading to noticeable improvements in school climate, culture, and student outcomes.

To recap, the ten components are:

1. Creating a Positive School Culture
2. Understanding Your Master and Bell Schedule
3. Knowing the Structure of Your School Building
4. Maximizing Your Resources
5. Staff Supervision Schedule
6. School-wide Classroom Expectations
7. Cafeteria Plan
8. Cell Phone Plan
9. Rewards & Consequences
10. Relationships with Students and Parents

By incorporating these components into daily practice, educators can create a positive, safe, and nurturing environment that promotes academic success, social-emotional growth, and a powerful sense of community among students, staff, and families. Ultimately, this book is a valuable resource for schools seeking to foster positive change and build a brighter future for all learning community members.

If your school needs support, please contact me by visiting my website. www.gregorynunleyjr.net